# A Diary of Prayer

*Daily Meditations on the Parables of Jesus*

BY
J. BARRIE SHEPHERD

THE WESTMINSTER PRESS
PHILADELPHIA

BOOK DESIGN BY DOROTHY ALDEN SMITH


*First edition*

Published by The Westminster Press®
Philadelphia, Pennsylvania

PRINTED IN THE UNITED STATES OF AMERICA
9 8 7 6 5 4 3 2 1

Library of Congress Cataloging in Publication Data
Shepherd, J    Barrie.
    A diary of prayer.

    1. Jesus Christ—Parables—Meditations.
2. Prayers. 1. Title.
BT375.2.S5        226'.806        80-27037
ISBN 0-664-24352-5

# CONTENTS

*And he told them a parable, to the effect
that they ought always to pray and not lose
heart.* (Luke 18:1)

## PREFACE

Many books have been written about the parables of
Jesus and it is with some trepidation that I attempt to add another
title to that library. This book, however, is not so much written
about the parables as it is around them. This is no scholarly piece
of solid Biblical research. Nor is it written in a preaching vein,
seeking to discover and expound precisely what Jesus meant when
he told these stories. My approach is neither critical nor exegetical;
not because I do not respect these methods. I have studied them,
used them, and taught them throughout my ministry, both in the
parish and on the college campus. This is a book of prayers; and
if I were to give any title to my method I should call it "medita-
tional." My attempt has been to permit each parable to speak to
me, in as direct and uncluttered a way as possible, in trust that,
through the Holy Spirit, my personal reflections of the impact of
each story may be a daily help to others who "feel after God and
find him."

I have ordered these meditations in diary form. This is
no new device. John Baillie's classic *Diary of Private Prayer* is my
most obvious model, and I have expressed my deep indebtedness
to Baillie in the introduction to my own earlier volume *Diary of
Daily Prayer.* As I suggested in that preface a diary is a personal
document. Therefore I have provided blank pages for each day on
which the reader/prayer is invited to begin to chart his or her own
spiritual journeys. It should be noted that the careful reading of
each parable is essential to the praying of these prayers.

There are so many to whom I am indebted. Largely to
my wife, Mhairi, whose patience and support made these pages
possible. I would dedicate this work, however, to my parents,
whose love, faith, and firm encouragement did much to set me on
the road I still pursue. I thank God for all who have helped along
the way.

J.B.S.

# DAY ONE

### On Parables

As I read again these stories
that you told, Lord Jesus, I am beginning to realize
just why you spoke in parables,
why you wrote no treaties,
delivered not one single dogma.
For as I read a parable a picture forms within.
I view a scene, a group of scenes,
and I am drawn inside to be a part of all I see.

You do not teach parables, far less preach them;
you weave them, Lord, and somehow I am caught
between the warp and the woof, entangled
not against my will, but as an act of sharing,
imagination, identification.
I see myself losing a coin,
finding a sheep, holding a feast.
I leave myself behind
and become a part of this great
finding, losing, hiding, hoping human race.
And then I see myself again more clearly
through the eyes of all humanity.

Your parables, Lord, do not teach
a lesson, inculcate any new theory for life;
they depict a situation and then
ask me to decide what will I do, or be, or give.
And thus I thank you
for the parable you gave in telling
parables.
     Amen.

*[handwritten annotations in right margin:]* to see myself reflected in the p. to learn of myself. to identify c̄ the "bad" + not the "good."

*[handwritten annotation at bottom:]* parable - how to live in response to O, in rltn to O, to see how O relates c̄ me.

# DAY ONE

## On Parables

Thinking again about your parables, Lord,
at the closing of this day,
I ask myself if there is any way
in which my life has been, *to show others who O is*
might be, a parable.

As I remember the delight
of those old yet living narratives,
their simplicity, their grace,
their directness and lack of all conceit,
their open-ended way of touching people's lives,
I think I understand.
To live life as a parable means *to live an "ordinary" life*
to craft it as a source of fascination
and of joy to all around;
as a clue, hidden yet intriguing,
to the great and final mystery of life;
as an invitation to a feast, to a wedding,
to a job, a challenge, to the dance;
as a way of posing questions that can cut through
to the basics—love and death. *– O is O of both*

Forgive me, Father, that there has been
so little of your magic
in my life today.
And craft me, like a living story,
that what I do and who I am
may sing out its own message,
the gospel of your bright, amazing grace
alive and active in this hungry world.

                              Amen.

DAY TWO / *Mark 4:3–9*

### The Sower

I look ahead across
the unsown field of this new day, Father,
and ask myself if I should even make the attempt to begin.
So much of the ground is already beaten down,
hardened by the feet of others,
unreceptive to whatever of myself,
of creativity and effort I might seek to plant there.
Even more of this day looks like rocky soil, Lord,
ready to produce results, but only for the instant—
those same old routine tasks which, though they must be done,
leave me no farther forward, and will have to be
undertaken all over again tomorrow.
Then there are the weeds,                    *I must be faithful*
groping up like claws to choke the life      *anyway.*
from any sense of purpose I might take
into this day, the weeds of worry,
of conceit, of self-protective fear, those weeds
that tell me all my efforts are for nothing
and will fade and die before this day is ended.  *There is promise.*
In this parable you paint a different picture.
You assure me there is good soil, deep loamy earth,
ready to receive the life I cast upon it.   *How much sowing*
You remind me to stop fretting about the harvest,  *can I do?*
to quit seeking guarantees, assured results,  *how much have I*
and to leave the future in your hands.        *done?*
You call me to the field
I have to sow this very day, and you promise
to tread the furrows by my side.
For this I thank you, Lord.
                    Amen.

*I can only put forth the seed, I cannot
cause it to grow.*

*All must have a chance to hear
whether they accept or not. The seed
is thrown not just on the good soil.
I wants to give us all a chance to
respond.*

# DAY TWO / *Mark 4:3–9*

*The Sower*

What kind of soil have I been today, Almighty Sower?
Your lively seed has touched me in so many ways;
but toughened by the treading of the years
I have seldom felt its impact
as it bounced off my calloused hide.
From time to time, perhaps,
there has been an impulse to do good,
to render thanks, to speak a word of prayer,
but the fierce heat soon withered it to dust.
Or again, I have initiated an act of genuine charity,
embarked upon some new and hopeful path,
only to find the weeds of timetable and schedule,
the daily demands that govern all my hours,
swallowing up my best intentions,
devouring them before they come to fruit.

Where was the good soil, Lord,
the ground that will bear fruit
in ways I cannot hope to see right now?
Was it in that letter that I wrote,
that honest deed, that friendly joke exchanged,
that momentary glimpse of loveliness
I stopped at, shared with a total stranger?
Might I have built your kingdom as I debated
with a friend, prayed for an enemy,
did homework with a child, admired a hamster
or a dinner cooked with care and faithfulness?

Forgive me, Lord, my barrenness this day,
and in your gracious wisdom bring
your secret seed to harvest
in my life.
                Amen.

# DAY THREE / *Luke 18:9–14*

### The Pharisee and the Publican

Lord, so much of my praying
never rises beyond the ceiling
of whatever room I happen to be in.
Just like this smug, self-satisfied Pharisee
who "prayed thus with himself,"
I too find most of my attempts at prayer
to be a tedious monologue,
not an open-ended dialogue in which
listening plays at least as large a part
as speaking.

Oh yes, I do address my prayers to you,
invoke your holy name at all
the decent and regular intervals.
But then I proceed to drown you out,
swamp your still small voice with all my wants,
my needs, my successes and failures,
my likes and dislikes, fears and prejudices.

Lead me, Lord, by quiet untrod paths, into
that full and open, simple conversation with you.
Teach me to listen patiently,
not fill my brain and crowding lips
with hurried, formal prayers or scattered thoughts.
Let me be afraid no longer of your truth, your judgment,
your call to lose myself in finding.
Free my praying from all the petty tyrannies
of wristwatch, diary, and calendar.
Help me to treasure this experience of timelessness,
these daily snatches of eternity given
to be sampled, foretasted in your presence.
And thus deepen me, and broaden me
for the work you give me to do.
                                          Amen.

# DAY THREE / *Luke 18:9–14*

## The Pharisee and the Publican

What was so special
about the prayer of this tax collector, Lord?
He didn't say much, really;
certainly nothing soaring, eloquent, or poetic.
It doesn't even say he changed his ways,
gave up on the betrayal of his fellow citizens.
Yet he "went down to his house justified."
He was a humble man, standing way in back,
not even presuming to raise his head in saying,
"God, be merciful to me a sinner!"

I find it hard, yes, tricky, to be humble.
The word has become confused, all mixed up with
false modesty and the like,
and we are no longer sure just what it means.
Humility, I would guess, stands right next door to honesty—
another neglected virtue of these times.
This tax collector seemed to know precisely who he was,
"a sinner." Simply that. He didn't make excuses,
compare himself with other persons
more outrageous than himself, didn't even
offer up the occasional generous impulse
in an attempt to balance his offenses.
He admitted who he was, then asked God's mercy,
and he got it.

Bring me, Lord, to such honesty.
Let me know myself as I am known within your holy presence.
Then may I find myself both humbled and restored,
not in public acts of fasting, tithing, and the like,
but by the steady, quiet transformation
that your Holy Spirit works in those who trust in you.

Amen.

DAY FOUR / *Matthew 13:47–50*

## *The Seine Net*

There is something full of hope
about a seine net, Lord.
Summers down in Maine
I see them set along the shore
by small commercial fishing boats
or by an enterprising lobsterman seeking bait
for hungry traps. They leave them there a day
or two, one circled line of floats upon the surface,
surrounded by the noisy congregation of the birds,
gulls, cormorants, and terns,
the entire fishing fraternity swooping,
diving, shrieking clamorous around
to claim their share of salty harvest.

To watch them haul a net, at last,
the busy dories rowing, circling,
the steady closing of the threaded purse,
is to share a great excitement,
the slow anticipation of a vast reward.
So much hope, so much hard work revolves around
that tightening circle of the sea.

So let your kingdom act upon my life today.
Brim it with hope, excitement,
the sheer exhilaration of a purpose shared
and labored hard and long for,
the trust that in your overflowing bounty
will be all the recompense
that I could ever dream of, far beyond
whatever glory I could ever hope to earn.

Amen.

# DAY FOUR / *Matthew 13:47–50*

## The Seine Net

We are so eager, Lord,
to sort and separate the good fish from the bad.
These "fish of every kind"
that gather in the net
are just not neat and orderly enough.
Who knows what evil influence they might have
on one another if allowed to mingle indiscriminately?
So, like these fishermen, we determine
our own kind of fish and toss away the rest.

Your parable warns against this, Lord.
You tell us there will be
a sorting and a judging to be done
but only in your own good time,
at the closing of the age.
And furthermore, it seems that we will not be
with the sorters, but with the sorted.

Forgive me, Father,
for all I have rejected out of hand
this very day.
Let me be truly grateful
that this mixed bag called "The Church"
was indiscriminate enough to welcome even me.
And teach me that, while I cannot hope
to fully comprehend your Day of Judgment in advance,
I can prepare myself for it
by judging less
and welcoming much more.
Amen.

# DAY FIVE / *Luke 15:8–10*

### *The Lost Coin*

This is a story, Lord,
with which we can all identify;
for while there are few folk in this day and age
who have ever lost, or found, a sheep,
lost money is a part of everyone's experience.
Nowadays, with inflation and all,
it would have to be at least a five-dollar bill
to merit all that sweeping
and that celebration.

Yet perhaps it was only a very small coin.
The footnote says a drachma,
worth today less than a quarter.
Hardly an occasion for a block party!
What then was the point of it all?

This tale suggests to me
that what we consider almost worthless
our God, the housewife of all creation, values
enough to turn that whole creation
upside down to find
and save and celebrate.

Reorder my own values, then.
Turn me upside down just like that simple home,
that I may see the lasting value of the little things,
the trifles, persons and concerns of no account.
Let me find in these
that which can help me to celebrate
your glory with my neighbors.
                                    Amen.

DAY FIVE / *Luke 15:8–10*

### The Lost Coin

One of my earliest memories, Lord,
goes back to days when pennies
and treats were few and far between—
back in England during World War II.
Mother had given me a penny
to spend in the local tuck-shop after school.
All through that day
my imagination glowed in delicious anticipation
of the decisions and delights that lay ahead.
Then, at four o'clock, I dug my hand deep
into my pocket, and the penny had vanished.
Lost, stolen, or strayed, it was gone.
I stood at the schoolyard gate and wept.
No matter who saw my tears—friends, enemies, teachers—
I sobbed in heedless disappointment.

Suddenly a passing stranger, an old man I recall—
probably in his mid-forties as I am now—
an old man stopped and asked what was the matter.
Pouring out pain, I shared my little tragedy,
whereupon he reached into his own pocket
and presented me another penny.
I don't remember what I bought, but
I never will forget
the grief and then the happiness I met that afternoon.
He probably forgot me in a day or two,
but his gentleness will live as long as I do.

Remind me, Lord, as I encounter those who weep,
how little things,
even the losing and finding of a penny,
can live, perhaps, forever in your holy economy,
the economy of sharing and of joy.
                    Amen.

# DAY SIX / *Mark 2:22*

*Wineskins*

How soon these wineskins age!
One day we are convinced that we are reaching out
to something new and daring.
Then, before we realize what is happening,
time has worked its deadly changes
and innovation has become tradition.
We seem to lose the knack for innovation
far too quickly. One breakthrough,
one new idea per generation seems to be
about the quota before we settle back
to do things as they have been done
since time began.

This wineskin of my life
seems to grow more and more into that pattern.
The creases, wrinkles, and folds set in so early.
And once they are established
day follows day, the weeks and seasons flow and merge
and little seems to change
except the numbers on the years as they flash by.
It's comfortable too
if you don't think too much,
or notice that those numbers slipping by
measure your life.

Is there still time, Lord,
time to launch out on something new;
time to change an old and hateful attitude,
a self-destructive habit;
time to mend a breach or heal a wounded friendship?
Grant me in your gracious providence, Father,
days sufficient to renew my old and creaking ways.
And let me begin this morning.
                    Amen.

DAY SIX / *Mark 2:22*

*Wineskins*

Where are those new wineskins
that can receive the vibrant life you pour upon us, Lord,
and be filled without the tearing,
creaking agony, the splitting of the seams?
The answer does not appear to be the church.
Bringing up a new idea in church
is too much like arriving at a cocktail party
in Bermuda shorts, and with a camera round one's neck.
Might this openness be found, then, with the young,
the sects, these new religious groupings
that spring up all round us nowadays?
They also seem to have their set and rigid ways,
ways which must be accepted without question.
New suggestions are quite clearly
most unwelcome in that company.
Might it be, Father,
that, just like charity,
new wineskins too begin at home?

Forgive me for the dryness of my own faith
with all its stubborn grooves and seams and cracks.
Make of it a new wineskin, soft,
supple, free to expand, to be rounded,
filled with a glowing spirit
that brings joy to the thirsty,
a smile to the eyes, and a song to the lips
of all who taste.
Brim me, Lord,
with your astonishing wine.
Then pour me forth for your gospel's sake.

Amen.

# DAY SEVEN / *Luke 14:31–33*

### *The King Going to War*

Lord Jesus Christ, this story
tells me something about you and the way
you undertook the challenge that you faced.
For you counted the cost,
made your plans carefully and well,
and even though the world around you
believed that you had lost the cause,
the victory was yours.

But that triumph still has to be completed.
Your plan of campaign continues to this day.
Therefore, when you numbered your troops for the battle,
I too must have figured in that reckoning.

Bring home to me this day, Lord,
this fundamental lesson of faith,
that somehow, in your wisdom,
my part is an essential one,
that each and every human life
has its own necessary role to play
in bringing in the kingdom of your peace.
When you counted the cost
and pushed ahead with all your plans
you counted also upon me, Lord.

Help me to live up
not only to the faith I have in you,
but even more so to the faith you had in me
in giving up your life in trust
that I would carry on the task
for which you came and fought and died.

                    Amen.

# DAY SEVEN / *Luke 14:31-33*

### *The King Going to War*

You never lied to us, Lord.
There was no deception, no shoddy salesmanship,
no hidden costs, fine print, where your gospel was concerned.
Our days are full of shady deals,
seductive offers, tricky bills of sale.
You made the price plain from the outset, warned us
if we had any doubts, any second thoughts,
not to begin.
You told us what the cost would be,
a cross, a life, no less than that.
And in return you promised life, your life for me
to die and live within me, to bring me to the self
that you created me to be before
the toil and smear of gain
and greed corrupted everything that is.

I too must count the cost,
the cost to you of what I do
and fail to do each day,
the cost to those around me of the way I live my life,
the cost to me of claiming your great name
and following in the costly way
you trod before me to the cross,
and finally, the cost of losing you,
of turning back, of making treaties with the wealth
and eager power of this world,
of losing your abundant life
in seeking cheap salvation of my own.
Lord, make me willing to pay the price of love.

Amen.

# DAY EIGHT / *Luke 15:3–7*

### The Lost Sheep

I wonder how he felt,
that one wandered sheep.
Did he realize that he was lost?
Or did he believe he was leading a movement,
pioneering a new and daring frontier?

Most sheep are not all that bright.
The only thing they do well is to flock.
They follow . . . follow . . . follow
whatever happens to be ahead of them
and smells vaguely like mutton.
Maybe this traveler was striking out on his own
for the very first time, breaking new ground,
searching for the grass that is always greener.
But then the turf gave out altogether
and the night came down and he discovered,
too late, that following was not so dumb after all.
Who would find him out here on the mountain?
Who would even miss him in that milling sheepfold?

At last a cry, and then a rush
and a hoist aloft onto strong shoulders
and such a cheering, bouncing ride back to the pen.
Why, it's almost as if this crazy shepherd has missed him!
Almost as if this laughing, racing shepherd
loves him like a child!
But then, who knows?
Maybe he does.

Thus, in your gentle guidance, Father,
permit me to wander off a little from time to time.
But never let me out of range
of your rejoicing shoulders.
Amen.

DAY EIGHT / *Luke 15:3–7*

## The Lost Sheep

Is your kingdom also
like being a neighbor, Lord,
knowing I am not really a part
of the main action, those major scenes of searching,
finding, homecoming,
yet finding myself swept up in the train of events,
summoned in, willy-nilly, at the end
to be a part of that splendid celebration?

I tell you,
it all did seem quite heavenly
as the evening wore on,
what with songs and dancing, wine and sweet figs,
and then story-swapping round the fire till daybreak.
I guess I felt as if I belonged,
as if I could relax and just be me
and be liked because of that,
loved because I was myself, no more—no less.
Yes, it was heavenly, almost as if
the angels were singing deep in my soul.
Could it be
that your kingdom has no crowds, Lord,
only communities?

Make me a part of your community this night.
May I rest in the peace of your kingdom,
and arise to rejoice in your service.
                                        Amen.

# DAY NINE / *Matthew 5:14–16*

### The Lamp Under a Basket

What more useless place to put a lamp
than under a sealed cover?
At times the church acts like a bushel basket, Lord.
You have lighted us a lamp,
a radiant source of light, a gift
that frees us from the fear of darkness,
reveals to us the power of your forgiveness,
shows us also where we stand
and the universal company we share,
even sheds its light ahead
onto the way that you would have us take.

But instead of following that way
we have taken your lamp, our light,
and walled it into buildings,
structures, laws and creeds and books
that in seeking to define the light
serve all too often to confine the light
and keep it for ourselves.
We tend the home fires, Lord,
and wonder why the flame needs so much tending.

What more useless place to put a lamp
than under a sealed cover?
What more useless way to treat your gospel
than to seal it off, away from those who stumble
in the dark, and thus create new darkness for ourselves?
For light cannot live long without
the full fresh air of freedom.
Help me this day, Father,
to lift at least one corner of the basket,
and so let your light shine forth
like the gleam of a new dawn.

Amen.

# DAY NINE / *Matthew 5:14–16*

### The Lamp Under a Basket

In letting my light shine forth, Father,
just how do I avoid practicing my
"piety before men in order to be seen by them"?
Your message was to do good deeds in secret,
not to parade whatever virtues
I might have before
an admiring world.

This is, to be sure, a delicate operation;
one in which I fail time and again;
to let my light so shine
that others see it and give you the glory.
For glory is at least a small reward for being good
and decent, and giving up so much.
And to have to wait until my "Father
who sees in secret will reward me"
can seem to be a long and lonely wait.

Teach me, Lord, the gentle
unselfconscious radiance of a candle,
the art of giving light
just by being what and who I am,
and thus, of shedding illumination
not on myself, but on your world, your Word,
your will for me and all your people.
Help me to burn quietly
and light a path away from self
toward the everlasting light
of Jesus the Christ.
                    Amen.

DAY TEN / *Matthew 25:31–46*

*The Sheep and the Goats*

From time to time we modern-day Christians
can be heard wishing we might have lived
twenty centuries ago and shared the special privilege
of knowing you in person, Lord.
What would it have been like to follow
along the highways, see your face,
hear your voice, feel the touch of your forgiving hands?
If only we could look into your eyes,
listen to your strong, yet gentle tones,
then it would be so much easier to believe;
or so we tell ourselves.

In this great parable of judgment
you tell us that we meet you every day;
that in each person who is sick or hungry,
in prison or in any kind of need,
you are there, waiting to be
recognized and welcomed.

"But what if we are tricked?" we say.
"There are so many crooks about today
who prey on honest people's charity
and take advantage of any indiscriminate and reckless
generosity." "True," you reply, "there are such people.
But which risk do you prefer:
the risk of being cheated of a little money,
time, or love, or the risk of denying me again,
of failing to recognize and know me for myself?"

Awaken within me this morning, Lord,
the realization that you wait to greet me
in every human relationship, in each
and every situation that faces me today.
                                        Amen.

DAY TEN / *Matthew 25:31–46*

*The Sheep and the Goats*

You ask so little of us, Lord,
that is what is remarkable about this parable.
The price of eternal bliss is not some heroic sacrifice,
the solving of a major problem of this weary world,
but rather, a piece of bread,
a cup of water,
an hour of sympathetic listening,
a night or two of common hospitality.
One does not have to be especially gifted,
talented, or wealthy to participate.
These are the kinds of deeds
that any one of us can perform,
acts that can form a part
of the daily round of living.

Perhaps we would prefer something much more strenuous:
one ultranoble deed, one single shining example.
Yet acts like these, fine though they be,
are not the most important.
What counts in life—
and in eternal life, you seem to tell us—
is this steady, everyday awareness by your people
of the needs of those around them,
the daily sensitivity and openness to the ordinary calls
to clothe your love in human flesh.
In this way,
so you tell us, we will meet you
and break bread with you, unknowing,
as those two did on the journey to Emmaus.
Amen.

# DAY ELEVEN / *Luke 7:31-35*

### Children in the Marketplace

These children in your story, Lord,
play a game that we all know,
that we polish and perfect as we grow older:
how to criticize and thus evade the issue.
"Why are Christians so contentious?
Why are preachers never perfect?
What about the instituted church with
its enormous assets, all those hypocrites
that fill up holy pews?
Who pursued the Inquisition,
planned Crusades, and burned the witches?
Why do Catholics act this way
and Protestants do that?"
Even Pilate, who demanded, "What is truth?"
dared not wait to hear your answer but rushed on
to wash his foolish hands in politics and law.
So we pick and poke and argue
oh so nicely from the sidelines, finding ways
we can avoid the searching question
that you pose by being you
and being with us.

Lord, when all the games are ended, you are here,
the living truth, in a cradle, on a cross,
beside the road, across the table,
in the marketplace where people come
to share their gifts and needs,
in this ordinary place where I begin another day.
As I go out today
into this marketplace of trading and relating,
preserve me, Lord, from silly evasive games.
Let me answer to your question
with my life.
                    Amen.

DAY ELEVEN / *Luke 7:31–35*

## *Children in the Marketplace*

When you said I must be like a little child, Lord,
I don't think this is what you had in mind.
What a profound difference there is, after all,
between being childlike and being childish.

I believe you must have meant that
we must catch again the unpretentiousness,
simplicity, the lack of pompous self-importance,
in a deeper sense the poverty of children.
That way, when we see the life you offer
we can grasp it with enthusiasm,
and with no reservations whatsoever.

My days
become so cluttered with childish nonsense, Father:
concerns about position and prestige,
the details of providing daily bread,
this endless grasping after a security
that I can never find this side
of the reality called death.

Receive back this day now, Lord.
Let the curtain of your night sweep away
all I have done in the pursuit of pointlessness.
Grant to me, here and now,
a clear and childlike vision of your purity and grace
to prepare me for my resting
and for the road ahead.
Amen.

# DAY TWELVE / *Matthew 20:1–16*

*Laborers in the Vineyard*

I wonder what the unions
would make of a deal like this, Father;
or management too, if they were asked
to follow this example.
It does seem a bit unfair, even to me,
that those who worked through the heat of the day
receive no more than these Johnny-come-latelies.
I suppose they did agree, at the outset,
to the rate of one denarius a day,
but it seems only human to resent others
receiving just as much for only
one twelfth of the work.
"Equal pay for equal work."
It's human nature, Lord.

But it's clearly not a part of your nature.
This story with its all too familiar scene
of hungry men—with families no doubt—
standing about all day waiting,
hoping to be hired,
tells me something of the nature of your grace.
Grace cannot be divided into more or less,
greater and smaller shares,
but is complete within itself,
and comes to all who seek it, soon or late.
You appear here, Lord, not as the judge,
the careful and precise divider of rewards,
but as the giver, rejoicing in the privilege
of shocking generosity, reveling in the wonder and surprise
of those who were recompensed beyond
their wildest dreams.

Surprise me, Lord, this day.
Shake me with the immeasurable wonder
of your grace.
         Amen.

DAY TWELVE / *Matthew 20:1–16*

### Laborers in the Vineyard

I see this scene played out
among my children every day, Lord.
"How come she got the biggest piece of pie?"
"Why should I do this,
when he had only to do that?"
"It's not fair,
it's just not fair!"

Such a silly, pointless game,
this business of comparing and contrasting;
of continually peering over the shoulder
of the other guy to see
if he got more than I did,
to make sure I have received
every single thing I am entitled to,
if not more.
It can rob the fun from everything we do,
since everything must be checked out
against everyone else
before it can be enjoyed, and by the time
we've finished checking
there is seldom much real joy left to be had.

Liberate me, Lord,
from this foolish, killing game.
Let me appreciate the miracle
of all your gifts to me
and accept them in the spirit they are offered in,
freely and with no strings attached.
Now, in this childlike gratitude,
I lay me down to sleep.
                    Amen.

# DAY THIRTEEN / *Luke 16:19–31*

## Dives and Lazarus

Dives was not such a wicked man.
He did not actually mistreat Lazarus,
order him removed from his gate,
refuse to him the scraps from his sumptuous table.
So long as it cost him no effort
he was quite content for Lazarus to be
what might be called a part of the household.
He may even have patted him on the head
once or twice as he passed in and out.
Clearly he recognized him, called him by his name.
Perhaps he felt that Lazarus,
by his very poverty,
heightened his own enjoyment of his lavish wealth.
And look at him now, begging to lick water
from that poor man's fingers as the dogs
once licked Lazarus' sores.

What did Dives do to deserve this bitter fate, Lord?
Might it have been because he accepted Lazarus,
knew him yet did absolutely nothing
to comfort him or ease his dreary suffering?

We no longer have the beggars at our gates, Father,
wouldn't even permit them there today.
But suffering and degradation have not vanished.
Persons still have to live on our scraps.
Persons still rake through the garbage cans
in every major city of this world.
If you condemned Dives, Lord,
what must you think of us?
We have removed the beggars from our gates
but not from misery.
As I go in and out this day
open my eyes and my heart.
Amen.

**DAY THIRTEEN /** *Luke 16:19–31*

*Dives and Lazarus*

In all your parables, Lord,
there is no one quite as wretched as poor Lazarus.
Yet he is the only character in all that lively
unforgettable crew to whom you gave a name.
We meet "the younger son," the "rich young ruler,"
the "publican," "Samaritan," and all the rest,
but only Lazarus is spoken of by name.
He cannot have been all that unique.
Such beggars, cripples,
the crushed and broken wreckage of humanity,
were everywhere to be seen,
as they still are in many cities nowadays.

Could it be that you gave his name
because, of all persons,
he is the least desirable to know?
We make a major effort, after all,
to remember and record
the important names, employers,
officials, influential contacts,
presidents of this and that;
but the names of beggars are not worth the effort.
We will never need to use them.
Even when we pass along a crumb or two
it is not necessary to know the name
of the recipient.

Help me, Father,
to cherish every child of yours as you do,
to treat them with that same unique respect
I savor for myself,
to share with everyone I meet
that dignity you gave to all of us
in sending us your Son
to be our Savior and our Lord.
                              Amen.

DAY FOURTEEN / *Matthew 5:25-26*

## The Defendant

Everyone seems to be suing everyone else, Lord.
It's almost as if we had lost
that special art of settling quarrels for ourselves
that is basic to the essence of community.
Or is it that we have discovered
yet another way to make money
out of discord and unhappiness,
to profit from misfortune and distress?
So much of life's hidden treasure,
of the wisdom that used to be discovered
in working things out together
through the simple structures of compromise
and cooperation, is forfeited,
lost in the tangled maze of litigation.

In times like these, Father,
your call to be an agent of reconciliation,
one who mends the torn fabric of trust
and mutual respect, seems especially urgent.
Teach me, therefore, in my home,
my work, my leisure time,
to seek with all the grace you have put in me
to dissipate tension,
to resolve conflict, to create harmony,
and to create anew the climate of your peace.
All this I ask through him
who has reconciled all things.

Amen.

DAY FOURTEEN / *Matthew 5:25–26*

*The Defendant*

This day,
like so many others,
has been punctuated by disputes
and disagreements, Lord.
Most of them minor,
and swiftly passing, to be sure:
the morning paper that arrived too late,
that impatient driver
in the early rush hour,
the boss, the secretary,
the clerk in the department store,
the spouse, the kids, the neighbor,
and the evening news;
yet all of them still clashes,
mental and verbal confrontations, at the least,
conflicts with my fellow human beings
that can spread with fatal ease
into a steady state of war.

What makes me so contentious, Lord,
so quick to judge,
so slow to share forgiveness?

Through this tale of The Defendant
I am learning that, like you,
I must be slow to anger,
swift in mercy, before it is too late;
before the prison house of enmity,
hostility, and vengeance closes
vast iron doors upon my days
and I am left to rage alone
forever.
  Amen.

# DAY FIFTEEN / *Mark 4:26–29*

*The Secret Seed*

Another day, Lord,
fourteen, fifteen more hours
of the usual routine, meals and chores,
tasks and duties, quarreling and making up,
all the familiar round of daily living
that goes on . . . it just goes on.

And is there seed in my life, Father?
Where are the shoots, the branches, and the leaves
that tell me I am growing,
that my grain is ripening?
Those same old petty weaknesses and sins
still dog my footsteps.
The same temptations cross my path
time after time.
I never did set out to be a saint,
but I did once dream, still do at times,
of maturing in the faith, coming to know
your closer, fuller presence as my Lord.

Perhaps I ought to be the last to know.
"The earth produces of itself."
Might there be processes within, your processes,
that work spontaneously and secretly?
For surely, if I turn my life over to you,
I no longer need to stop and feel my pulse,
measure height and weight and strength continually.
You will bring forth the fruit in its due season.

So take this new day, let the gentle rain of prayer,
the rich and fertile nutrient of your word,
the sunlight of my fellow human beings,
so feed my bones and blood and being
that I might grow unknowingly
to that promised fullness,
the measure of the stature of the fullness of Christ.

                                        Amen.

DAY FIFTEEN / *Mark 4:26–29*

*The Secret Seed*

What happened to your church, Lord Jesus?
Nearly two thousand years have come and gone
and where have we, your "body," come to?
More Christians, to be sure, than ever before.
But what kind of Christians are we,
fighting among ourselves,
squabbling over property and propriety,
competing in those worldly games—
success, statistics, marketing, publicity—
securing the solid walls of our own fortresses
while your lost children live in hovels
and know squalor and disease?

Grant me a glimpse tonight, Lord, of your own vision.
Let me see, within this vast and worldly institution,
the many branches of your tree of life,
the multitude of quiet deeds of love
known only to the two or three, and to you,
the clumsy, yet still effective generosity
that even yet can mend a wound, relieve a pain,
comfort human sorrow, and work to free the captives.

Remind me, Father, of that great host
of ordinary men and women
who labor here and there, high places and low,
not necessarily to "bring in the kingdom,"
but to share at least a taste
of the grace, the hope, the promise they have received.
And teach me, not to chafe impatiently,
but instead to try to number my own life
with those who play their part,
and playing it give thanks.
                         Amen.

# DAY SIXTEEN / *Matthew 13:44*

### Hidden Treasure

Lord, so many of these parables
share this basic element of hiddenness.
They remind us that your kingdom is not obvious,
does not present itself in all its glory
the moment we walk into church,
open up the Bible, or kneel in prayer.
Your kingdom is more apt to be surprising,
like a game of hide-and-seek
when someone leaps out from behind a tree
and we dissolve in laughter
or in tears.

We search for the kingdom.
We strive hard to achieve its coming,
at times by almost superhuman feats of discipline,
hard work, and sacrifice.
Then, all of a sudden, the veil is lifted,
and for an instant, or at the most an hour or so,
we know it, feel it, taste it,
at the heart of a song, the ending of a book,
deep down an avenue of snowy trees,
or in an evening's quiet conversation.
Time is forgotten, self left behind.
We are with you.

I thank you for these hidden things,
the moments that surprise, the secret depths
that hide below the surface
of your wonderful, mysterious creation.
Let me not be so preoccupied
with the busyness of this day
that I forget to watch for, to be open to,
the treasures you have hid along the way.

Amen.

DAY SIXTEEN / *Matthew 13:44*

*Hidden Treasure*

Was this man some kind of crook, Lord?
Did he really deal in complete honesty
with the owner when he bought that field?
I should guess he kept the letter of the law
but not its spirit.
One thing he did, however.
When he found the thing he wanted,
he acted. No hesitation or delay.

You come to us so many times like this, Lord.
You show us life,
hold life out toward us
in your pierced and bleeding hands,
and we say, "Maybe." We say, "What about the price?"
We ask, "Give me until tomorrow to decide."
Then the gift is gone,
the moment fled, and we may never find
that chance to live again.
I suspect, indeed I'm almost sure,
you will return, there will be other opportunities.
But the more we put you off,
the less likely are we ever to decide
to seize that moment, buy that field,
pull back the groaning hinges of the door
that blocks the way to life in you.

Forgive my timid caution, Lord.
Show me how to seize each and every treasured moment
that you offer for my living of these days.
Amen.

# DAY SEVENTEEN / *Luke 15:11–32*

## The Prodigal Son

So much has been preached
and taught, spoken, written, prayed
about this well-worn story, Lord,
so many sermons, lectures, poems, even films,
that I wonder if anything new can be said
about The Prodigal.
What if nothing new needs to be said?

We are obsessed with newness today, Father,
constantly looking for newer, better ways
to do things, make things.
And within the realm of things
this may well be to the good; after all,
we still need new inventions, ways to grow more food,
house and educate more people, fuel our vast society
without poisoning ourselves in the process.
But in the realm of ideas,
of dreams and human aspirations,
sometimes the old can never be improved upon.
If someone finds a new and improved Shakespeare,
Michelangelo, or Bach, I for one
will not stand in any line to see or hear.

Help me, Father, to listen again this morning
to the old, old story of a father and his sons:
the foolish son—the faithful son,
the humble son—the jealous son,
and the father, oh that father!
running down the road on weary, tottering legs
to wrap his long-lost boy within his arms
and cover him with tears of gladness;
then, in loving patience, reasoning with the older son
to bring him also smiling to the feast.
I hope the story ended in that way.
And since you are the father, Lord,
somehow I'm sure it will.
                    Amen.

# DAY SEVENTEEN / *Luke 15:11–32*

*The Prodigal Son*

"And there he wasted his substance with riotous living."
Such a powerful, descriptive phrase!
A phrase which, though discarded in all
the new translations, will never die within
the treasure-house of the imagination.
"Riotous living"—what wild, illicit pictures
these rich words conjure up, scenes far from the everyday
experience, I would guess,
of most modern-day church members.

Still, while "riotous living" may not be
what most of us go in for, the wasting of substance
is quite another matter.
We too have come into an inheritance,
a world of vast resources and astonishing beauty,
art, culture, institutions, and traditions
that can, if tended carefully, evoke
the very best in human nature.
But we create a throwaway society,
a world of litter, landfills, toxic wastes,
a·marketplace where our precious human ingenuity
is channeled to the making
and the selling of a host of useless products,
or construction of the mad machines of war and megadeath.
Just like that lost boy, Father,
we are learning what it's like to seek nourishment
from pig swill in a trough.

Bring us to ourselves, Lord.
Send us stumbling back along the once familiar road
to home, that place where we can, even yet,
take up again a decent and responsible life,
a serving life within your household
and under your unchanging care and mercy.
                                        Amen.

DAY EIGHTEEN / *Matthew 7:24-27*

### The House Upon the Rock

We often call you "carpenter," Lord Jesus,
but forget just what that title means.
You must have fashioned mangers, cradles,
tables, beds, and doors, the stuff of many parables.
You knew exactly how to build a house
and brace it to endure the storms and blasts.
Houses built on sand, Lord,
are not uncommon, even today.
I knew an island house in Maine,
squatter-built on no-man's-land,
just at the edge of the beach.
It stood for ten or fifteen years until,
the winter before last, such a storm blew
out of the northeast as had not been seen
in recent memory, and the place was gutted, washed clean,
left an empty tilting shell upon the shore

Lives can be like that, careers, marriages too,
balanced on an eggshell of forgotten lies, half-truths,
deceptions—self and others—that have lasted somehow
but will never make it through the testing days to come.

I watched an island carpenter rebuild that shattered cottage,
set concrete footings deep down onto rock,
restore the place until it looked
just as it did before the storm but stood
much stronger, firmer to the waves and wind.
My life could use such skill and craft, Lord Carpenter,
to help me sink foundations that will never shake,
foundations resting on the Rock of Ages.
Be my master builder, Lord,
this day and every day.
                    Amen.

DAY EIGHTEEN / *Matthew 7:24–27*

## *The House Upon the Rock*

Luke records this story
with a slightly different setting, Lord.
He describes the builder digging
long and deep to reach the solid rock.

It is not always easy
to build well and for the future.
Time, finances, declining human energy
lead me, all too often, to begin to build
without the proper preparation, hoping against hope
that I will be lucky,
that the storms will pass me by.

Yet you tell me in this story
that I will be tested, soon or late,
and that the outcome will depend on what I do
right here, right now,
on the bases I have laid in this very day, now closing.

Forgive me, Lord, the sandy soil
of easy comfort, selfish pleasure, cheap entertainment,
defensive, timid, even hostile living,
on which I waste so many priceless hours.
Bring me back, again and again, to your Word,
your truth, your wisdom, and your love,
that one foundation that can bear the weight
of all my foolishness and failure
and stand firm beneath me
till the end of time.
                    Amen.

# DAY NINETEEN / *Mark 4:30–32*

### The Mustard Seed

Your church began
like this, Lord Jesus,
twelve men and one of them a traitor,
and a group of faithful, wise, and understanding women.
What a microscopic grain of seed!
A mere speck of dust in the eye
of the imperial elephant that was Rome.

And, just as you said, Lord,
that tiny seed had to taste death,
to know earth upon its lips,
the savage ways of beasts,
both animal and human,
before it could germinate, sprout roots,
send forth green shoots and leaves,
and finally bear fruit,
fruit which, in its turn, was sown
along the furrow of this cruel world.
All this until the tree that is your church
can shelter every creature
in its lofty shade.

Remind me, Father,
as I enter upon this day,
that I too am a part of that vast rooted, growing life.
And grant that I might share today its task
of sheltering and nurturing the weary
and the needy of this world.
Through Jesus Christ, the Lord
and sower of the seed,
I make this prayer.
                    Amen.

DAY NINETEEN / *Mark 4:30–32*

### The Mustard Seed

As I review the words and acts
that punctuate the moments of this day, Father,
I can see that much of what I have done
and said across these hours
can also be compared to that mustard seed.

The long testimony of the ages
in saga, story, and song relates how one
seemingly insignificant action
can set events in motion that will lead, in time,
to quite enormous and unforeseen consequences.
A single act of trust,
of faith, of generosity,
or of quiet self-denial can so transform a life
as to touch thousands in its blossoming.
While one solitary deed of fear
or hatred can bring despair and doom
to entire families, even whole societies.

And every now and then,
in your wisdom, Lord,
good can result from evil.
That soldier who planted a rough cross
two thousand years ago had no idea
what rich, explosive seed he set
within the soil of history.

Lord, let me rest now knowing
that the seeds I have sown this day
will grow or die within the royal purpose
of your overruling providence
and your grace.
                    Amen.

# DAY TWENTY / *Matthew 25:1–13*

### The Ten Virgins

I guess I just do not understand
Eastern wedding customs, Lord.
Why those virgins? What on earth were they waiting for?
Those lamps, too, did they all have to be burning?
Surely five lamps would have cast light enough for everyone.
And what was that bridegroom doing
hanging around in the dark until midnight
on his wedding day?
And, while I'm asking questions,
don't you think those "wise" virgins
displayed precious little of what today
we would call "a Christian attitude of sharing"?

Are you trying to tell me
in this story, Lord, that a time will come
when it will be too late for me:
too late to look for help from other people,
too late to take last-minute, emergency measures,
too late for anything but a tight-shut door
and the final word to "Go away"?

I've seen this happen between people, Father.
And I know I've missed the boat with you
a time or two before now,
those times when a moment comes and goes for love
and never comes again, no matter
how we pound the heavy door of time.

Lord, wise or foolish, let me recognize
your coming and your call this day,
and be ready to go with you
where you lead.
                    Amen.

*The Ten Virgins*

How did those wise
and prudent virgins feel
hearing their sisters crying outside the door?
Did they congratulate each other
on their foresight, their single-minded dedication
in refusing to share their valuable oil?
Or did they wonder just a bit,
know at least one flash of remorse and pity,
feel a momentary urge to push
the stern bridegroom to one side
and fling that door wide open?

Perhaps I'm trying
to make more of this story
than Jesus meant to put into it, Father,
but parables are for playing with,
or so I've always suspected.

I ask myself,
If I had been there,
which side of the door would I have been on?
I don't believe
I would like to have been
one of those oh-so-prudent persons
for all their precious oil.

Father, forgive me
if in this day now ending
I have been so prudent as to neglect
the needs of others, foolish or otherwise.
Forgive also the foolish, imprudent ways
by which I have neglected to prepare
a way for you in the wilderness.
                         Amen.

# DAY TWENTY-ONE / *Luke 14:16–24*

*The Great Feast*

If I were invited
to a royal wedding, Lord,
I wouldn't turn it down for anything.
After all, how many of those
does one get to attend in one lifetime?
I can see myself now, one of the honored guests,
with a ticket bearing the royal crest,
a reserved seat in the VIP area,
away from all the noise and smell of the crowd.
Just think of the prewedding parties,
the receptions, champagne and dancing,
lights and color and music.

Only one problem arises,
what kind of gift could I bring?
It's hard enough nowadays finding something
for a common or garden wedding;
something affordable, yet not too cheap.
But as for the wedding of a king's son . . . !
Maybe that's why the guests in your story
all made their excuses.
Maybe they really couldn't afford to attend, knowing
that the only gift you wanted
and could ever accept was a heart
broken open and ready for service.

So let me come to the feast
of this new day, Father,
not looking for a good time or a splendid show,
but willing to offer the gift
of my own self to you
and to your people.
                    Amen.

# DAY TWENTY-ONE / *Luke 14:16–24*

*The Great Feast*

Looking back over today, Lord,
I recall the many invitations I have turned down:
invitations to dinner or to debate,
to dialogue, to danger, even to the dance;
invitations that appeared to contain
too much of a claim, a demand;
invitations that might take me away
from my work, my family, my own self.

It's not always easy,
this turning down, but I have to do it
if I am to keep my life and sanity intact.
Yet some of these requests
may also contain a cry for help,
for company, for a shoulder to lean on,
a hand to grasp, a listening, sympathetic ear.
Am I also turning down invitations to participate
in life and in lives,
in pain perhaps, but also in great joy,
in all the tangled skein that makes up
full and honest human relationships?

Teach me, Father,
how to refuse and how to accept,
and the wisdom to know which to choose, and when.
Your Son refused a crown
and, instead, accepted a cross.
Let his example guide me
as I move in trust and hope toward
your final invitation to the wedding feast
of the Lamb.
                    Amen.

# DAY TWENTY-TWO / *Matthew 21:28–32*

*The Two Sons*

I recognize myself
and many fellow Christians in that second son
who said, respectfully, "I go, sir,"
and did not.
We are so free with pledges,
promises, and the like.
The average Sunday morning hymn
contains enough commitment to rebuild the world
if those who sang would live it out next day.

Small wonder people call us hypocrites, Lord.
We seem to feel that witnessing consists
in speaking your name as often
and as loudly as possible in public,
rather than in living your life for the sake of the world.
People hear too many words today, Father,
pushing, selling, tricky and deceptive words.
We need to get your message out
from the commercial spots
and into the daily news.
We need to follow you in being more
than just a spoken word:
a living word, a working word,
a word that can be seen and touched
and known across the barriers
that keep folk from each other.

So teach me and my fellow Christians, Lord,
to be more sparing, cautious of the words we speak,
and much more certain that we follow through
in actions that fulfill and go beyond
what any words alone can tell.
Amen.

DAY TWENTY-TWO / *Matthew 21:28–32*

### *The Two Sons*

To be completely honest, Father,
neither of these two boys seems to be exactly perfect.
The first, while he does the job eventually,
refuses in such a brusque and surly way
that I suspect he caused his father
grief, pain, and even anger.
The second, though he answers
sweetly and with due respect,
seems then to get caught up in other things
and falls down lamely on his promise.

I know this same experience
with my own youngsters, Lord.
And while I must agree that, in the end,
results mean far more than words,
yet attitudes are basic too. Best of all
would be the child who responds in willingness,
and then cheerfully completes the task.

Once in a great while this happens in my family
and then I know that I am truly blessed.
It happened once for you, I know,
when that one true Son of God
lived all his days according to your will
and in communion with you.
What a blessing and a cause for joy
that must have been to you, such joy in fact
that this world still resounds with your rejoicing,
such a blessing that it reaches to this very day
and graces all I undertake
with your forgiving mercy.
                    Amen.

# DAY TWENTY-THREE / *Luke 12:42–48*

## Faithful and Unfaithful Servants

How easy it would be, Lord,
to be that "faithful and wise steward"
dispensing bread to the hungry,
love to the lonely,
power to the dispossessed;
how relatively simple this could be
if I only knew precisely when
you were due back to judge, redeem, and reward.

As things are,
the days stretch into years
and then into centuries, and still
the wicked prosper, goodness fails, as usual,
to find its merited reward.
While, in the meantime,
there are bills to be paid, a future
and a family to be provided for,
and a cruel world to be survived somehow.
Couldn't you give a hint, at least
the occasional clue to keep me on my toes?

Ah, but what if you have already come!
The judgment is in process here and now,
and I can be condemned, or yet redeemed,
in every act and moment
of this new day spread before me.

Master, renew my sense of stewardship.
Prepare me for your coming, that, soon or late,
this day or at the closing of all days,
I might know joy in welcoming
my Lord's returning home.
                    Amen.

# DAY TWENTY-THREE / *Luke 12:42–48*

*Faithful and Unfaithful Servants*

Trouble is, Master,
we are not really given this kind of authority.
If only I did have control
as steward over all this world's resources,
then it would be a far less tricky matter
to see that all received their portion "at the proper time."
The goods are there, or could be,
to ensure that no one starved.
In fact, no one need ever hunger nowadays,
but distribution seems to be the stumbling block.

This human race is so caught up in other things,
the race for power in all its many forms,
we do not have the time, the brains, the energy
to dry the tears of starving children
and stop their sobbing with good, nutritious bread.
Surely this parable is directed at the mighty,
at those in control, and not at little me.

Yet where does this control begin?
After all, I do possess a reasonable share
of time, brains, and energy.
I have a vote, a bank account,
a voice, a pen, a job, more than enough to eat.
I have been set as steward
over more than one fair portion of this world's estate.
Forgive me, Lord, for giving in so easily,
for abdicating willingly the power
I have been entrusted with.
Show me how to be your faithful servant,
not just for the sake of that reward, or from fear
of punishment, but in and through the overflowing
of your saving love.
                    Amen.

# DAY TWENTY-FOUR / *Luke 11:5–13*

### The Friend at Midnight

I guess we have to work at prayer too, Lord.
Just like the householder in this parable,
or that poor widow with the unjust judge,
we need to keep on asking,
making our requests until they finally are granted.
It's almost as if we have to earn results in prayer
by way of dedication and persistence.

Somehow, though, that does not seem quite right.
The grace of God is surely not a gift
that can be worked for.
Your love and mercy, we are told, is freely given
for the asking and receiving,
free like manna in the desert or like sunrise,
and cannot, must not be earned.
Besides, Father, if the whole point of this tale
was to encourage persistence, you would be presented
in a most unattractive light—the reluctant neighbor,
who will not stir himself to aid
a friend in need.

The clue would seem to lie in "how much more."
If we can persuade such ugly human characters as these
to respond to our needs by persistent nagging,
how much more readily and willingly and lovingly
will you, our Heavenly Father, grant to us
the wishes of our hearts.
So may I base this new and opening day
on the amazing generosity of your grace
and not the empty merit
of my own striving.
                    Amen.

# DAY TWENTY-FOUR / *Luke 11:5–13*

## The Friend at Midnight

"Ask, and it will be given you."
But, Lord, it's never really just that simple;
at least not in my life, or in other lives I know.
The parable asks us if an earthly father
would give his child a snake when he asks for a fish.
But what if the child, in ignorance, asks for a snake?
In fact, we do not always get what we ask for,
and some of the things we do get,
some of the accidents, diseases, and misfortunes
that come upon your children, appear difficult to justify
on any grounds whatsoever.

Are we to say that cancer,
sudden accidental death, disaster,
blind injustice, poverty are really what is best
in your divine, eternal wisdom;
and that someday, somehow we will understand?
I believe I will understand,
but I cannot accept that agony
is part of your eternal plan for humankind.
Some suffering we bring upon ourselves.
We inflict much more on others
by our rejection of your royal law of love.
But natural disaster and the like
seem far beyond such ready explanations.

What we do have is your love;
your love made flesh in one who suffered with us,
suffered at our hands and for our sakes.
This is a love that, even in the mystery of pain
and fear and anguish, loves us still,
bears pain with us, shares the full weight of agony,
and goes with us down all the bitter ways
right to the end and then beyond.
                              Amen.

# DAY TWENTY-FIVE / *Matthew 25:14–30*

### The Talents

Yes, Lord, I realize that talents
in this narrative
does not really mean what we call talents,
should be translated as a certain sum of money—
call them dollars, pounds, dinars.
But might it, still and also, mean our talents—
the gifts, skills, and abilities
you set within us at our birth?

Certainly these are all given to us
from your creating hands.
One cannot earn, or learn a talent.
And, just as certainly,
they are by no means evenly distributed.
Just like the talents in this parable
some of us have five, others two,
and some have only one,
or so it seems.
True to the story also we can choose to invest
our given talents, to expose, explore, express them
as we relate to our fellow human beings.
Or we can bury them, repress our gifts
for fear of being criticized or, even worse,
of not proving the best.

As I go forth into this day, Father,
let me use whatever gifts you have entrusted
to my keeping to the fullest,
highest range of their potential.
Let me do this, not from any sense of superiority
or gifted arrogance, but out of a true spirit
of humble, Christlike sharing.
Thus will I be your "good and faithful servant."
                                        Amen.

*The Talents*

Father, you have invested
so much of your precious capital
in me, and in my fellow Christians.
You have entrusted to our keeping
the living word of your only-begotten Son,
the written word of your two holy Testaments,
the sacred acts of Baptism and of the Lord's Supper,
the tradition and wisdom of twenty centuries of saints.

Yet too often we take all this treasure
and transform it into something as dry as dust,
or as narrow and uninviting as a hole dug in the ground.
We reduce the dancing word of life
into a list of chilly dogmas
and lifeless "Thou shalt nots."
We water down the stunning,
demanding encounter with the living Christ
into a mass-produced excess of overwarmed emotion.
In so many cautious and protective ways, Lord,
we attempt to preserve your gift of gospel
for ourselves and folks like us.

Judge me tonight, Lord,
review with me my talents and my use of them
before it is too late to learn.
Set free your gift of grace within my living.
And let it lead me out into creative investments
of my life and my love in the building
of your kingdom.
                    Amen.

# DAY TWENTY-SIX / *Luke 20:9–18*

### The Vineyard

Did we kill you, Lord, for this?
Behind all other motives given and guessed at
did we crucify you because we knew who you were
and wanted to claim your inheritance?
We kept asking about your authority.
Surely after so many parables, miracles,
glimpses and snatches of truth we realized
where your authority came from:
direct from the Father himself.
But then all that power was set within reach,
in our hands if we only could stretch out
and seize it. No more wrestling with conscience
or living with guilt and remorse.
No rules, obligations, and duties
to cramp our free style.
"Here is our chance to get rid of God's rule
once for all, to claim the inheritance,
all of the wealth of this globe for ourselves.
And all that it costs is one life."

We did just what you said we would do
when you told us this parable:
nailed you to a tree in the heart of the vineyard
you built. And we thought, "God is dead.
Now this place is completely our own."

How wrong could we be?
For death set you free to come to us still
with a claim that is stronger than ever before.
"Look how I love you, died for you, live for you,
strive for you, weep and rejoice with you,
bring you to life, if you only will choose it."

Let me choose life today, Lord.
Send me forth to your vineyard to tend it
and mend it with care and in peace.
                              Amen.

*The Vineyard*

When you told this parable, Lord,
you knew, without any doubt or question,
just what was going to happen.
There is no way around
this simple, lucid, and effective story.
It tells of your imminent death
and the reasons behind it.

Why did you tell it? I wonder.
Was it designed to arouse alarm,
even panic and rage in the hearts of all those
who were secretly plotting your downfall?
It certainly must have had that effect.
Was this parable meant as a threat of reprisal
to those who would do away with you?
To be sure, it does carry a warning.
Were you, perhaps, letting us know,
those who heard you then,
those who hear you today,
that you went to your death open-eyed;
not cheated or tricked or deceived,
simply rejected?

I think it must have taken
an overwhelming courage to fling
the facts of betrayal and conspiracy
back into the teeth of your murderers,
confident that not even the gates of hell
could prevail against God's reconciling love
that was, and is alive in you.

Forgive me, Lord, the petty betrayals
and cowardices of this day, now past,
and lend me something of your boldness
when you put me to the test.
                    Amen.

# DAY TWENTY-SEVEN / *Luke 13:6-9*

*The Fig Tree*

If there is one sin
you denounced more than any other
in your parables and teachings, Lord Jesus,
it is the sin of fruitlessness.
You describe it in many ways,
through different images,
but the basic failing is that of doing nothing,
of allowing the gift of life
with all its varied possibilities
to dry up and wither away.

The reasons can be many—
laziness, lack of imagination,
or just plain fear, the paralyzing inability
to bear the necessary risk
that must accompany each act,
the risk of failure.

At times I get the feeling, Lord,
that you would prefer the rogue or crook,
any kind of positive, active sinner,
to the bland and empty apathy of fruitlessness.

Grant me, Father, the courage to take risks
in this new day; to thrust my roots
deep into the soil of human suffering
and injustice, my branches high toward the sun
of your sustaining light and love.
And thus to bear you strong
and sweet and nourishing fruit
with all the life that's in me.
                    Amen.

# DAY TWENTY-SEVEN / *Luke 13:6–9*

### The Fig Tree

This Christian life you call us to, Lord,
is so often portrayed by preachers and the like
as being basically a matter
of avoiding sin and evil.
It's as if we had been issued new white garments
and success depended solely upon
maintaining their spotless condition.
The problem with such a negative approach
is that it leads to fruitlessness.
We become so preoccupied with keeping ourselves pure
that we dare not risk the rough-and-tumble
of feeding hungry people, righting wrongs,
housing the homeless, visiting prisons.
So many of these people are in flagrant violation
of your holy laws, and we fear
any compromising contact with such folk.

This fig tree story suggests to me, Lord,
that it's not what we haven't done that counts,
but what we have.
The tree had done no harm, after all.
It hadn't poisoned anyone.
It simply stood there, took up space,
and gave no fruit; and for that,
it was condemned.

Teach me again, Lord, the lesson
of your own life, of your friendships with the sinners
of society, that life will not be discovered
in the avoidance of sin alone; but only
in the wholehearted pursuit of love,
wherever it leads and whomever it leads me to.
And forgive me, Lord, if
and when I fail.
       Amen.

# DAY TWENTY-EIGHT / *Luke* 10:25–37

### The Good Samaritan

"And who is my neighbor?"
That crafty lawyer!
He tried to trap you into a debate, Lord,
a learned discussion, to be sure, citing precedents
and laws, chapter and verse and line,
about precisely what might constitute a "neighbor."
It's only reasonable, if we are to be commanded
to love one, we had better know exactly
what a "neighbor" is and is not;
and, while we're at it make quite clear
the specific obligations that can be expected of one
vis-à-vis said "neighbor."

This is a strategy we all employ, Lord.
We learn from early age the ways to postpone,
by debate, the taking of any action whatsoever.
It's so much safer that way.
So long as we are wrangling over
the finer points of "neighbordom" we do not have
to do a blessed thing about that body
lying wounded by the road.
So we join our seminars, discussion groups, and such
to try to puzzle out just what our faith
is calling us to do today, and all the while
brothers and sisters die of hunger,
deprivation, and despair.

Help me to know the limits of debate, Father,
when it is time to stop and think, discuss and plan,
and when to put a speedy end to all deliberation
and to act in faith and in response
to crying human need.
                    Amen.

# DAY TWENTY-EIGHT / *Luke 10:25–37*

### The Good Samaritan

You never really answered
that lawyer's question, Lord.
He wanted you to tell him whom he had to love;
and whom, by implication, he could hate,
or neglect as unimportant.
You did not tell him, as I used to think,
he must love everyone, even the lowly
and despised Samaritan.
Quite to the contrary,
the Samaritan—the neighbor in your story—
was the helper, not the helped,
the lover, not the one in need of love.
You showed that lawyer
just how easy it can be to love, to be a neighbor;
so simple and uncomplicated that even this Samaritan,
completely without the benefit of Jewish law
and practice, could act neighborly
without a moment's hesitation or debate.

To be a neighbor, then,
means not to count the cost, not to worry
that this lone abandoned body might only be a decoy
for a hidden band of robbers,
not to calculate that if you stop to help,
the long delay might cost you precious moments
in the temple, or wherever you are bound.
To be a neighbor is to see and feel the pain of others
and to share it in the name of one
who bore our sorrows for us
that we might share the joy he knew
in losing life, and finding it again.

                    Amen.

# DAY TWENTY-NINE / *Matthew 18:21-35*

### The Unforgiving Servant

"Pay what you owe."
Four harsh and threatening words
that spell out doom, not just to this poor servant,
but to everyone who hears them.
"Pay what you owe."

What do I owe, Father?
What might be the magnitude of my indebtedness
if I were ever asked to pay you back?
What value should I place
on the first breath of springtime,
the golden palaces of fall?
What could I pay for music and for art,
for soaring mountains and the restless sea,
for this rich heritage of learning and tradition,
the many daily comforts that surround me,
this body which, for all its aches and pains,
has served me well across the years?
What do I owe for love
that tendered me through infancy
and childhood, bore with me in adolescence,
supports and struggles with me still
in countless ways through family and friends?
How much should I pay back for faith,
a church to serve in and be served by,
a table at which everyone is welcomed and is fed,
a book in which to trace the path of living,
a Lord who will not let me fall forever?

You know I cannot pay, Lord,
and in your grace you tell me to forget the debts,
accept your gifts, and live in them
with joy and gratefulness.
                    Amen.

# DAY TWENTY-NINE / *Matthew 18:21–35*

*The Unforgiving Servant*

Forgiveness is the meaning of this story, Lord.
As I read I am compelled to ask myself this question,
Whom do I not forgive?
To whom in my life, even this day,
have I been like this unforgiving servant,
grabbing all your grace, and giving none away?

So much of daily living
can be built on grudges, hurts, and old resentments.
At times it seems as if the closer I am to someone,
the more difficult it is to forgive.
With colleagues among whom I work,
neighbors, those with whom I pass my leisure time,
fellow members of societies and clubs,
even churches, especially churches,
forgiveness is a rare, endangered species in my life.
There are the faceless grudges too:
against politicians and the poor, the folk we punish
in our prisons by the grim conditions
in which they have to exist.
Can we forgive the old for being old and wrinkled,
for reminding us of what we will become?
Can I forgive myself, Lord,
for not living out my dreams,
for years of quiet failure and defeat?

Deliver me this night, Father,
from the prison I have built around my life,
this jailhouse of resentment and old fears;
and let me taste the freedom of forgiveness,
the liberty of living in the kingdom of your grace,
in Jesus Christ.
      Amen.

# DAY THIRTY / *Luke 12:13–21*

### The Rich Fool

What a fool he was, Lord,
that wealthy farmer with his bumper crop;
not a thought for the poor, the needy,
or even for his tax deductions.
Nowadays, with United Way, the Heart Fund,
the dollar in the plate on Sunday mornings,
people know better than to be so foolish.

And what about those barns he planned to build, Father?
I guess we all build barns of one kind or another.
We build the barn of influence and self-esteem,
always seeking to further our own prosperity,
knowing the right people, being seen
with them in all the proper places,
trying in everything we say and do and wear
to project our own importance,
attractiveness, or success.
Or there is the barn of things we construct
from day to day, the latest gadget
or the newest toy, properties and real estate,
all the solid stuff we gather round us
to amuse us or protect us from the storm.
Yet something, somewhere keeps telling us
that self and stuff are not enough.
We see, without admitting it,
that far from us consuming them, possessions in the end
will consume us by their demands
on our time and energy.

Tear down my self-protective, foolish barns,
and let me spend this day out in the open,
my sole security in this,
your promise, "I am with you."
Amen.

# DAY THIRTY / *Luke 12:13–21*

*The Rich Fool*

Yet another barn I build, Father,
is the tall barn of tomorrow: that rainy day,
that crunch, that possible disaster up ahead
to be provided for . . . just in case.
Again there are the golden years,
those blissful, far-off days
when having amassed a vast collection of fine things
I can at last relax and just enjoy them.

Which, of all these tomorrows, am I building for?
Is it that tomorrow which may come,
either disaster or those longed-for days of ease?
Then what about that other tomorrow,
the day that will dawn sure as sunrise-sunset,
the day when things no longer help,
when self is not enough, when life comes to full stop
and I stand on the threshold of eternity?
Will it be enough to say, "I built some barns"?
Then I fear you will respond,
"Were there no lives you touched and healed,
no hungry children that you fed, fellow sinners
with whom you shared a word, a meal, a moment?
Did you create no beauty, ease no pain,
conquer no evil, brighten no single solitary place
of darkness and despair?
Did I die to buy you time to build a barn?"

Which tomorrow have I been building for today?
Free me, Lord, from all the foolish fears that bind me
to myself, my precious things.
Let me place this night and my tomorrows in your hands,
for you are my beginning and my ending,
my one eternal hope in Jesus Christ.
                                    Amen.

DAY THIRTY-ONE / *Matthew 13:33*

*The Leaven*

I wonder why you said
the woman hid the leaven, Lord.
If she really meant to hide it,
she put it in the worst possible of places,
for very quickly everyone would know
just where the leaven was concealed
by the rising of that solid lump of dough.

In another sense, however,
perhaps she did hide it after all.
That piece of leaven was never seen again.
Its effects were overwhelmingly visible,
but the yeast itself was lost,
forever now a part of something
greater than itself.

How can the church get lost
in this way, Lord?
How can we so completely hide ourselves
within the needs and hurts,
potentials of this all too solid world,
that finally the heavy, sticky mass
will really be transformed;
your people not a self-supporting enclave
within a hostile territory,
but a radiating source of power
which permeates the entire creation
until everything is leavened,
lightened into life, and sings your praise?

Help me to lose myself this day
as leaven in the lump.
                              Amen.

DAY THIRTY-ONE / *Matthew 13:33*

## The Leaven

As I reread this parable tonight, Father,
I remember my own father
and his baker's shop.
Late every evening
he prepared for the next day's rolls,
kneading and pounding the solid,
heavy clay-like lump of dough.
Then when the consistency was just perfect
he dropped it with a thud
to the foot of a large wooden barrel
and tearing off a piece of yeast
flung it on top and retired to bed.
At five o'clock next day—
Behold the miracle!
An overflowing tub of light
and fluffy stuff for making breakfast rolls;
crisp, brown, and featherweight they were,
the finest in the town.

So let the magic leaven
of your word, your healing presence,
work through the sleeping hours
upon this solid lump of clay
that I would offer for your service.
And may I rise refreshed, renewed,
and filled to overflowing, brimming
with the effervescent power that can make my day
a blessing and a source of strength
and daily bread to others I may meet.
                                    Amen.